WHAT YOUR
CAT NEEDS

—— By Liz Palika ——

A Dorling Kindersley Book

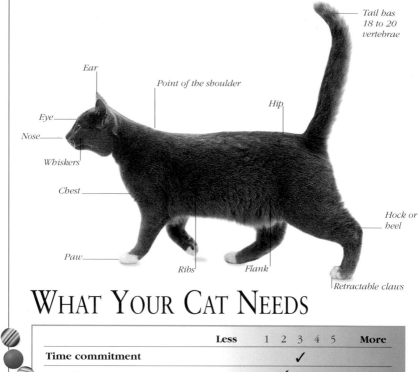

Tail has 18 to 20 vertebrae

Ear

Point of the shoulder

Hip

Eye

Nose

Whiskers

Chest

Hock or heel

Paw

Ribs

Flank

Retractable claws

WHAT YOUR CAT NEEDS

	Less	1	2	3	4	5	More
Time commitment				✓			
Exercise			✓				
Play time				✓			
Space requirements		✓					
Grooming (depending on breed)			✓	✓	✓		
Feeding				✓			
Cleaning up				✓			
Life span					✓		
Good with kids 5 to 10			✓				
Good with kids 10 and over				✓			

CONTENTS

FOREWORD BY BRUCE FOGLE, DVM

Cats! We have a curiously ambivalent attitude towards them, almost a love-hate relationship. Our love of their esthetic perfection draws us to them. After all, the cat is, in her looks and movement, the most gloriously sublime of animals. Her large eyes compel you to return her gaze. Her silken coat demands caressing. She moves with the fluid grace of flowing lava.

Everything about the cat reminds us of how downright klutzy we are. A calming purr, a head rubbed against your leg; my blood pressure is dropping just thinking how relaxingly beautiful cats are.

But there is the other side of the coin. Out of European cultural history has come the tradition that cats are untrustworthy, deceitful, agents of the devil. Well, hogwash! The cat is what she is, no more, no less: a self-sufficient, amiable descendent of the North African wild cat, a species that found living in human communities good for her own survival. We found it useful to have cats living with us, but we have frequently misunderstood them.

Speaking as a clinical veterinarian, my impression is that pet owners understand their dogs because we share so many social behaviors

with dogs. But we have more difficulty understanding our cats. This should not be surprising. Our pet cats have only recently evolved from the solitary hunting wild cat.

In other words, cats evolved to think of themselves first. They do not have a pack mentality the way dogs, birds, and rabbits do. But they do retain the sociable nature of being a member of an extended family, and that is at the crux of our relationship with them. Raised from kittenhood with us, a cat develops a loving, affectionate relationship with her human family. She doesn't just tolerate our company, she needs and enjoys it.

Cats bring true nature into our homes and our lives. They give us a window on the real world, the wild world of animals. They are not deceitful, but rather attractively honest in their feelings and emotions. They remind us of the real values of life.

We owe them something in return: to treat them as cats, supremely self-sufficient hunters, not as people in disguise. We should respect their emotional as well as physical and environmental needs, and protect them from the dangers of a crowded, congested human environment, where there are many unnatural challenges and risks. Getting off to the right start is the best way I can suggest to do that. This little book helps set you on a proper course toward what I hope will be a fruitful, rewarding relationship with your beautiful feline friend.

There's a little bit of the wild cat in every domestic cat. Understanding and respecting your cat's nature will help you both build a better relationship.

WILD CATS AND YOUR CAT

There are wild cats all over the world in a variety of habitats: forests, jungles, grasslands, mountains, and savannas. All wild cats have certain needs. One of these needs is lots of space, since most species of wild cats are happiest living the solitary life. All cats must also have meat in order to survive, so a population of wild cats is dependent upon the abundance of prey and a territory in which to roam to find that prey. In addition, wild cats need room and security to raise their young, and a healthy environment in which to live.

Most species of wild and domestic cats share some similar characteristics. With a few exceptions, they have a body that is longer than it is tall, a long tail for balance, and retractable claws. The housecat purring on the foot of your bed, the leopard sleeping in a tall tree in Africa, and the puma resting on a cliffside in the Sierra Madre Mountains of North America are all very much alike.

All wild cats are exclusively carnivores and are efficient hunters. Their prey differs, of course, but one similarity is their reliance on catching their own dinner. Unlike wild (or domesticated) dogs, cats are rarely scavengers. Whereas a wild dog might visit another animal's kill, steal an old, partially decayed carcass, or raid the garbage, most cats prefer to catch their own prey. Household cats mimic this desire for fresh food. Many will not touch, never mind eat, food that is left over from the last meal. This desire for fresh food could very possibly be a survival technique; the cat who eats fresh food is less likely to be poisoned by spoiled food.

Your domesticated cat will mimic other behaviors shown by her wild cousins. Even if your cat's food arrives on schedule every day, many cats like to hunt their food. They may slink down the hall, peek around a corner, sneak up on the food dish and then pounce. And in play, your cat's favorite games will be those that mimic hunting behaviors.

DOMESTICATING THE CAT

Cats have always been useful to us, although in a very different way than most other domesticated animals. Rather than teaching cats to do tasks for us, as we did with dogs and horses, we have domesticated cats to do what they have always done: hunt rodents. Because rodents can spoil so much food so quickly, and because rodents often carry parasites and disease, the cats who hunted these pests were prized.

The ancient Egyptians worshipped cats. Cats were a direct representative of their gods and were to be protected, coddled, and worshipped. When an important person died, his cats were buried with him. Air holes and secret passages were built into the tombs. When the cats found their way out, the person's spirit was said to have escaped as well and ascended to the great beyond.

Unfortunately, the worship of cats in Egypt did not spread to other parts of the world. In some places during history – especially in Europe during the Middle Ages – cats were associated with witches, or were considered bad luck and were killed on sight. But the ancients paid for their misunderstanding of cats. Without these feline hunters, the rodent population quickly multiplied, carrying the plague – the Black Death – across much of Europe and western Asia.

Luckily for us today, cats have again become pets and companions. Medical researchers have now stated what cats owners have always known: Cats are good for us! Cat owners tend to handle stress better than people who don't have any pets. Cat owners have lower blood pressure and recuperate from serious injuries or illnesses better than non-pet owners. What a wonderful tribute to our pets!

Cat owners never believe that myth that our cats don't need us – they need as much attention and affection as any pet – but cats also have an air of independence that we can admire. Cats need us without being needy, and love us without being sentimental. In addition, cats have a special mystery and grace that has long fascinated us. It's a thrill to have a tiny tiger on the couch. There's no denying it.

LET'S GO SHOPPING

Are you going to be adding a cat to your family? Before you bring home your new friend, you will need to go shopping. As any cat owner can tell you, there are hundreds of things you can buy for your cat. These are just the basics.

FOOD AND WATER DISHES

These dishes must be easy to clean. Stainless steel dishes work very well, as do ceramic ones. Avoid plastic dishes; many cats develop acne on the chin after repeatedly rubbing their chin against plastic dishes.

Ceramic dish   *Stainless steel dish*

GROOMING SUPPLIES

If your cat is shorthaired, you will need a metal comb, a soft brush, a slicker brush, and a pair of nail trimmers. If you have a longhaired cat, you'll need a metal comb, a pin brush, a rake, and possibly a matt-splitter.

Comb   *Slicker brush*   *Pin brush*

Litter box liner

LITTER BOX AND SUPPLIES

You will need a litter box, litter, and a scoop. There are many different types of litter boxes. Choose one that will be big enough for your cat and easy for you to clean. Choose a litter that won't track out of the box and one with little or no dust and no fragrance (read the label on the bag or box). Find a good spot for the box before you bring your cat home.

Scoop

CARRIER

You will want a sturdy carrier so your cat will be safe on her ride home and whenever she needs to travel. A plastic carrier is fine, as are canvas pet carriers. There are many different models on the market. Choose one that will be big enough for your cat, easy for you to carry, and that will keep her safe.

SCRATCHING POST OR CAT TREE

You will want to teach your cat to scratch on her scratching post or cat tree instead of the furniture, so choose a post or tree that you won't mind having in the house. Posts are usually carpeted or wrapped with sisal, and can be found in many different colors. Make sure the upright part is tall enough so that your cat can still stretch up to scratch it when she's full grown.

MORE INFORMATION

Cat ownership isn't always easy, even though cats have been our companions for thousands of years. However, there is a lot of help available to you. Your local book store, pet supply store, or library will have books and videos to help you. You may want to pick up a book or two on caring for and training your cat. You may also want to talk to your veterinarian, who can answer your questions about cat health and behavior.

FUN AND SAFE TOYS

Later in this book I'll talk about the importance of play, both as good exercise for your cat and to strengthen your relationship with your cat. But right now you will want to pick up a few toys while you're shopping.

FISHING POLE TOYS

These are small poles with a toy (such as a ball, a feather, or a piece of fur) on the end of the line. These toys are made for you to play interactively with your cat. She will not play with them unless you make them move.

BALL TRACK TOYS

These toys are round like a donut, with a top and a bottom and a ball in between. There are usually holes or openings where the cat can see the ball and where she can get her paw in to bat at the ball. When she bats the ball, it goes around and around the circular track. Some of the balls are hollow and you can put catnip in them. Once a cat learns how to play with this toy, it can be left out and she can amuse herself. However, be aware that cats do not play with these toys for a long time, because they're just not as interesting as toys that you make move in unpredictable ways.

TOY MICE

Cats are attracted to mice, and, throwing political correctness to the wind, seem to prefer mouse toys covered with fur. Pet supply stores have all kinds of mice toys for your cat, including remote control mice, fur mice, catnip mice, and more. While these toys may look a lot like mice to us, your cat won't be fooled. But she'll probably enjoy them anyway.

CATNIP

Catnip is an herb in the mint family. The dried leaves and flowers are very attractive to most cats (although not all), and cats will roll in it, pounce on it, eat it, and just generally make silly fools of themselves. Catnip can be found in toys or sold by itself. Sprinkled on the cat's scratching post or cat tree, it makes them more tempting than your couch or chair leg.

SAFETY FIRST

Toys should be fun for you and your cat, but think about safety when you buy them.

- ○ Don't buy toys with tinsel or metallic strings that could be swallowed.
- ○ Make sure the toys don't have any small pieces that could be torn off, chewed off, or swallowed.
- ○ Don't get toys with jagged or sharp edges.
- ○ If the cat might chew on the toy, make sure it's made of safe materials.
- ○ Think about how your cat will play with that toy. Is it safe?
- ○ Some toys may be safe for interactive play with you, but not safe to leave around all the time. Feather toys are a good example. Remember to put them away when you're not there to supervise.

MAKE YOUR HOUSE SAFE

Remember that saying, "Curiosity killed the cat?" Unfortunately, there is some truth to that old cliché. Your new kitten or cat will be very curious about her new surroundings and will want to explore, which is fine as long as you have made sure your house is safe for her.

First of all, make sure the house is secure; that your new kitten or cat can't escape through a torn window screen or a loosely latched door. If your cat gets out in the first few days, she won't have any idea where home is and could get lost. A fall from a window can also kill a cat. Don't believe those urban myths that cats can walk away from ten-story falls. They can't. Look at your house from a small cat's point of view, not yours. That means close the flue in the fireplace, look for weak or loose spots in all of the screens, check the bottoms of all the doors to the outside and look at the attic and the basement.

Throughout the house, put baby guards over all unused electrical sockets. In the kitchen, make sure cleansers, drain cleaners, and other chemicals are put away behind a latching cupboard door. Child-proof latches work very well. You may want to put away some of the breakable (or dangerous) things you store on the counters and shelves. You can teach your cat to stay off the kitchen counters and out of the china cabinet, but when you first bring her home she won't know the rules. In the living room, put away any breakable

The trash is full of dangers for your kitty. Keep your garbage in a can with a secure lid.

Cats do chew on plants. Keep your plant and your cat safe by moving your houseplants out of reach.

collectibles (at least for a while) and knick-knacks. Tuck electrical cords up and away, and do the same with the phone cord.

Make sure all types of medications, vitamins, and supplements are safely put away. Craft supplies, including yarn, string and thread, need to be put away so that the cat doesn't wrap herself up in them or try to swallow them. Other supplies, such as paints, resins, and clays, should also be stored out of the cat's reach.

Houseplants can also be a problem. Ivy and philodendron, both very common houseplants, are toxic to cats. So are many common bulbs, including crocuses, daffodils, narcissus, tulips, and lilies. However, cats can get into trouble even without eating house plants. Some cats decide that potted plants make wonderful litter boxes. If you can, hang as many houseplants as possible above the cat's reach. Cover the dirt in the others with crumpled aluminum foil or large, heavy stones. This will deter house training accidents.

THE HOMECOMING

Bring home your new kitten or cat when you will be able to spend some time with her. A Friday evening is great if you will be able to stay home Saturday and Sunday. You will want to get to know your new pet, and your cat will need to get to know you and bond with you. The only way this will happen is if you spend time together in the house and, hopefully, in the same room.

Use your new carrier to bring the cat home, and make sure everyone in the family resists the temptation to open the carrier on the ride home. A scaredy cat is a terrible weapon in a moving vehicle! Even if the cat is crying, leave her in the carrier until you get home and all the doors and windows are closed. Then you can let her out.

Don't force your new kitten or cat to cuddle with you right away. Cats have a very strong urge to run from danger (this is called the flight instinct), and if your new cat feels worried, afraid, or cornered, she may fight you to get away. So instead of making her cuddle with you, just sit on the floor outside of the carrier and open the door. She'll eventually come out on her own. Let her explore a little.

INSIDE OR OUT?

Is your cat going to be an inside-only cat? If so, wonderful! I applaud your decision. Are you still undecided? Let me share my experiences with you.

I grew up in a cat-loving family. We always had a cat or two, and the cats lived inside with free access to the outside. As a child, I didn't realize that the cats were always being replaced. But they were. We had new cats all the time.

When my husband and I got married and moved into our first home, of course I got a cat. That cat, Pywacket, was hit and killed by a car before she was two years old. Our next cat, King Lear, was killed by a coyote in our own backyard when she was less than a year old. I am sorry to say it took the loss of those two cats for me to learn that the outside world is very dangerous for cats. Our next cat, Tigger, lived inside only, had a full, interesting life, and lived to be seventeen and a half years old before she died of old age.

The outside world is a dangerous place. There are cars and poisons and careless neighbors and automatic garage doors and wild animals and neighborhood dogs and tougher, bigger cats and broken glass and many other things that can hurt or kill your cat. The average life span for an outdoor cat is three to five years. The average life span for an indoor cat is twelve to sixteen years. Unless you can provide your cat with an outside run that is fenced in all around, top and bottom, please don't let her out!

When she comes to you, pet her softly and talk to her quietly but don't grab her and hug her. If she curls up on your lap after a little exploring, feel privileged. You have been accepted!

Have other family members follow this same procedure for several weeks – yes, weeks! If you have brought home a young kitten, you will be accepted very quickly and the kitten will soon be curling up on laps or shoulders for loves and cuddles. However, if you have adopted an older kitten or an adult cat, give the cat time to bond with you. One of the worst things you can do at this point is push the cat or force her to be close.

ALL ABOUT LITTER BOXES

TYPES OF BOXES

When you go shopping for a litter box, you may find yourself overwhelmed by all the different styles of boxes and types of litter. It can be confusing. There are plain boxes that are really just big, deep plastic trays. If you have a shy cat or a cat who demands privacy, you may want to get a covered box. There are boxes that clean the litter – either automatically or manually – by running a rake through it and depositing the waste in a container for disposal. There are also boxes with grates under the litter (almost like a flour sifter) so you can pick up the grate part, shake the litter through, and get rid of the waste. As a longtime cat owner, I have found that the simpler cat boxes work best for me. They are easy to keep clean, and for both my cats and me that is the most important thing. Therefore, I use large, plain plastic, rectangular litter boxes.

LITTER CHOICES

Plain clay litter was the first commercial cat litter offered for sale. It is still one of the most popular litters sold, although many now have deodorizers added to them. Clay litters absorb moisture and help prevent smell. Some clay litters track easily and can cause a mess outside of the litter box. Other clay litters can be quite dusty. These boxes must be scooped daily and cleaned regularly (at least once a week for one cat, more often with multiple cats) with all of the litter being scooped or dumped, and the box cleaned and refilled.

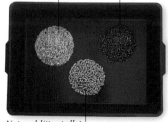

Clumping litter

Clay litter

Natural litter pellets

Clumping litters do exactly what they say: When moisture hits them, they form lumps that encapsulate the moisture. The clumps can then be scooped out of the box several times a day. Because this clumping material is often very fine, tracking out of the box can be a problem. Also, if a cat is used to clay litter, she may not recognize the clumping variety as litter and may refuse to use it. There are also litters made out of dried corn cobs, chopped into pieces, litters made from recycled paper or sawdust, and many others. You will just have to look at them, compare their good points with their weak point, and decide which will work best for you and your cat. Read the labels. Is the litter dust-free? Does it have added deodorizers? (Some is OK, but too much fragrance can offend your cat's delicate sense of smell!)

PERFECT PLACEMENT

Try to find a good spot for the litter box before you bring your new cat home. Ideally, the box should be in a place where the cat can get to it without difficulty, where you can get to it easily to scoop and clean, and yet where it's out of the way for family activities. If there is too much activity around the box, your cat may be hesitant to use it; many cats require privacy! Once your cat is used to the location of the litter box, changing it can be difficult (your cat may go looking for it in the old location and have an accident), so find a good spot for the box and leave it there.

HOW MANY BOXES DO YOU NEED?

If you have only one cat and an average-size house, one litter box will work just fine. However, if you have a large house or a two-story house, you may want to have two boxes – one at either end of the house or one upstairs and one downstairs.

If you have more than one cat you may have to add more boxes, because some cats refuse to share a litter box. Some cat owners put out one box per cat. Actually, although this sounds like a lot of work, it's not a bad idea. If a cat has a health problem, it's much easier to see the evidence of it in the litter box when each cat has her own box.

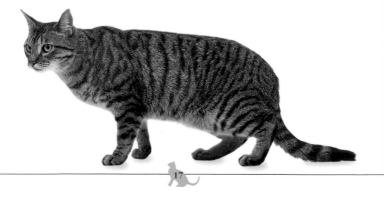

CAT MEETS BOX

When you first bring your new kitten or cat home, put her in the litter box right away but don't be surprised if she jumps right back out. That's fine. Take her back there in a half hour or so, though, and every half an hour until she uses the box. Over the next few days, take her to the box first thing in the morning, before you go to bed, after she eats, and every once in awhile throughout the day.

When she relieves herself in the box after you've put her there, very quietly (don't disturb her!) praise her, "Good kitty! Good!" When she jumps out, you can pet her and praise her more enthusiastically.

If you see that she's making trips to the box on her own, you can gradually decrease the number of times that you take her there. With most cats this house training is a very easy process. A newly adopted adult cat just needs to know where the box is, and once she's figured that out and her way around the house, everything should be fine. If you have brought home a young kitten, though, keep taking her to the box a few times each day. That positive reinforcement for using the box is never a bad thing.

KEEP THE BOX CLEAN

The most important thing to remember about litter box training is to keep that litter box clean! Even though it is most cat owners' least favorite chore, it is the most important one. More cats have accidents because their box is dirty than for any other reason. Keeping the box clean is much easier than trying to retrain a cat who has decided that her box is filthy and refuses to use it.

For one cat, all litter boxes should be scooped once a day at minimum. For a two-cat household, scoop at least twice a day. Clay, corn cob, and recycled paper litter should be completely changed once a week, with all of the litter disposed of (in a sealed garbage bag), the box cleaned, and then refilled. Some clumping litters can be used for an extended period of time as long as they are scooped regularly and additional clean litter is added. However, let your nose be your guide. If the box is beginning to smell to you, it's even worse for your cat. Change the litter and wash out the box!

IF IT'S WORKING, DON'T CHANGE IT

Cats are creatures of habit and dislike change. Once you have set up a litter box that your cat likes and is using, don't change anything. Don't get a new litter just because it looks like it might be better. Your cat doesn't care that it's the newest thing available, and she may just decide that it's not what she wants. Maintaining the status quo is your goal here.

Many cats are quite picky about their litter box and its location. But the biggest problem has to do with litter box training accidents. Once a cat decides to stop using her box, litter box training behavior problems can be quite difficult to correct. It's much better to find out what works, what pleases the cat, and then stick to it. You just don't mess with the litter box!

FELINE NUTRITION

Your domestic cat is a carnivore, just like her wild cousins. The prey a cat catches must supply all of the nutrition needed for good health. Because of this, wild cats eat more than just the muscle meat of their prey. They eat just about every part except the bigger bones, the heaviest fur, and hooves or nails. This variety, which often includes the contents of the prey animal's stomach, helps keep the wild cat strong and healthy.

Domesticated cats today don't have to hunt for their food, but the commercial food your cat eats must still supply all of the nutrients needed for good health. Good nutrition is made up of several important components, all of which must be present in your cat's food. If one or more is missing, your cat's health will suffer.

○ **Vitamins** are organic compounds vital to life. They affect the metabolism of food, growth, reproduction, and a thousand other bodily processes. They are found, in varying amounts, in the foods your cat eats and are added to commercial cat foods.

○ **Minerals** are inorganic compounds and are just as important as vitamins. Minerals work in conjunction with other minerals, vitamins or other compounds, such as amino acids or enzymes.

○ **Amino acids** are needed for growth and healing, as well as other bodily functions. Amino acids are found in proteins, and, in turn, help the body metabolize proteins.

WHAT IS TAURINE?

Taurine is an amino acid that works with the electrically active tissues (such as the brain and heart) to help stabilize cell membranes. Taurine aids in the movement of many minerals (including magnesium, calcium, sodium, and others) in and out of cells, which helps generate nerve impulses. Taurine has been used to treat seizure disorders, heart disease, and high cholesterol.

Several years ago veterinarians were seeing many cats with heart disease, vision problems, depression, and low fertility. Eventually many of these problems were linked to low levels of taurine in the commercial cat foods the affected cats were eating. At the time, taurine was being added to the food, but for whatever reason the cats were not metabolizing it.

Today, taurine is being added to commercial cat foods in a more easily metabolized form. Deficiencies are rarely seen now, and when they are, it is usually because of other problems, not because of the commercial foods.

○ **Proteins** can be complete or incomplete. Complete proteins contain all of the amino acids needed for good health, and can be found in red muscle meats, fish, dairy products, and eggs. Incomplete proteins are good foods but do not have all of the amino acids needed by the cat's body, and can be found in beans, soybeans, nuts, and grains.

○ **Enzymes** are protein-based chemicals that are found in every cell of the body and work to cause biochemical reactions that affect every stage of metabolism. Most enzymes work with a co-enzyme, usually a vitamin, to cause the needed reaction.

○ **Fat** is necessary for good nutrition. Fats help metabolize the fat-soluble vitamins (D, E, and K). They also supply energy.

○ **Carbohydrates** are sugars and starches. They produce fuel for the cat's body. Complex carbohydrates (grains, rice, potatoes, and pasta) are intricate conglomerations of glucose (sugar) molecules.

Commercial cat foods that are labeled "Nutritionally balanced and complete" contain all of the components needed for good health. However, not all cat foods are created equal. To find out what is in your cat's food, read the label carefully. How much protein is listed? How much fat? In what order are the ingredients listed? Is the first ingredient a meat? It should be; after all, your cat is a carnivore.

Keep in mind when you're shopping for cat food that you basically get what you pay for. If you are buying a cheap cat food, your cat will be getting cheap nutrition. And most cats have a very difficult time thriving on cheap foods. The result is dull, dry coats, itching and scratching, and lack of energy. The more expensive foods have better quality ingredients that are more easily digested, as well. That means you can feed your cat smaller portions, because she is able to use more of the nutrients in the food. And that makes the expensive foods much less expensive, meal for meal. The difference can show up in the litter box, too, as many of the cheaper foods have more filler ingredients. Since so much of what goes into cheap cats foods is unusable by your cat, much of it comes out the other end.

DRY FOOD OR CANNED?

Most cat foods are sold in one of two forms: either small, dry, formed pieces or canned. Dry food is usually grain-based with meat and other ingredients added. This food is much cheaper than canned foods, stays fresh for quite awhile in the cupboard, and the scraping action of the food against the cat's teeth helps prevent tartar build-up on the teeth. Most cats will eat dry food quite willingly.

Canned foods are meat-based and may or may not have any other ingredients added. Canned food is very moist, often with eighty percent or more water. To get the same amount of nutrition as dry food, canned food is very expensive. The softness of the canned food will not help keep teeth clean at all, and in fact, can lead to more tartar build-up. Most cats are very enthusiastic about canned foods; the moisture and high meat content are very tempting.

A diet based on dry food with a small amount of canned food in a separate dish is usually acceptable to both cats and their owners. The cost is reasonable and the cat will enjoy her food. A little canned food is especially helpful in making sure your cat gets enough water. Of course, fresh clean water should be available to your cat at all times, as well.

A combination of wet and dry food, with treats offered sparingly, will keep your cat's teeth healthy while still making sure she has enough water in her diet.

WHEN, WHERE, AND HOW MUCH TO FEED?

Many cat owners keep a dish full of dry food and let their cat nibble whenever she wants. If you have only one cat and know how much food is set out each morning, this is OK. But if you have more than one cat, it could be a problem. If one of your cats gets sick, one of the first questions the veterinarian will ask is if your cat is eating. How will you know? In addition, some cats will guard the food bowl and will not let a smaller or subordinate cat near to eat. A much better solution is to offer each cat her own bowl of food twice a day, and when the food is gone or the cat walks away from the bowl, pick it up. (Never leave wet food down for more than about fifteen minutes. It spoils very quickly, and smells bad even faster.)

Most cats will thrive when fed twice a day, morning and evening. Give your cat her food in a quiet place away from the noise and activity of the family. If things are too active around her, your cat might not eat or might not eat enough. Feed her in the same place every day.

All cat foods will have feeding instructions on the label. These are guidelines as to how much to feed, but the actual amounts will vary from cat to cat. If you are feeding the recommended amount but your cat is crying for more and is thin, feed her more. If you are feeding the recommended amount and your cat is getting a bit chubby, cut back on her food a little. Ultimately, how much to feed will depend upon your individual cat's body metabolism, age, and activity level.

DIET EXTRAS

SHOULD YOU FEED YOUR CAT PEOPLE FOOD?

Commercial cat foods are developed for cats; the food we eat was not. In fact, cats eating a high-quality cat food are probably eating a better diet than many people! If you would like to feed your cat people food, keep in mind that anything you add to a commercial cat food diet could potentially upset the nutritional value of that food. For example, if the food you are feeding is balanced with the proper amount of calcium (as high-quality foods are) and you add a food that is high in phosphorus, you can inhibit calcium absorption in her system. This could lead to many problems, including rickets, slow or poor growth, and poor healing.

Cats are also much smarter than we give them credit for, and if you regularly give your cat people food she may decide to eat that instead of her cat food. You could end up with a spoiled cat with behavior problems. She could insist on jumping on the table while you're eating, stealing food from your plate. Your cat may decide to raid the kitchen cupboards or take food from the counters. When you couple the cat's intelligence with her athletic abilities, a cat who decides she wants people food could be a real problem!

CATS LOVE TUNA

Cats love tuna fish, especially the tuna packed in oil. However, feed tuna to your cat very sparingly; give it only as a special treat. Veterinarians and researchers have found that tuna fish can actually be addicting to some cats. They will literally go hungry rather than eat something other than food with tuna in it. That's why so many cat foods contain tuna. If you read the labels, even foods labeled "beef and rice" may have tuna fish (or simply fish or fish meal) farther down on the list of ingredients.

Any diet that focuses on one particular ingredient is not good nutrition, so feed tuna sparingly. In addition, if your cat might be a tuna junkie, make sure you read the cat food labels and avoid foods with tuna in them.

GIVING YOUR CAT TREATS

Treats are like kitty candy, and should not be given in excess. Just as with people food, the amount of treats you give your cat each day should not be enough to upset her daily diet. Many commercial cat treats are high in sugar, salt, artificial preservatives, and/or calories, and too much can disrupt the nutritional value of your cat's food. Treats can be used for training your cat, though, and I'll discuss how to do that later in this book. Treats can also be used to give your cat medication when she needs it, or at least to soothe both your nerves after the medication has been given.

SUPPLEMENTS

Supplements are extras that you add to your cat's diet. These could be vitamin and mineral tablets, a little canned food added to the dry food, or a little bit of yogurt. High-quality cat foods are nutritionally balanced, and anything added to that food in large amounts has the potential to disrupt the nutritional balance. However, the nutritional needs of all cats are not the same. Therefore, supplements that are given wisely (never in excess) should not adversely affect your cat's health. Some possible supplements could include:

○ **A vitamin and mineral supplement:** It should include all of the vitamins and minerals, including calcium and zinc.
○ **Yogurt:** A teaspoon full per cat per day is a good source of amino acids and is good for cats with flatulence. The live active cultures in yogurt are good for the digestive system.
○ **Brewer's yeast:** This is often recommended for flea control, but is not really effective for that purpose. However, it is actually very good nutrition by itself.
○ **Chicken broth:** This can make dry food more attractive, and is good food by itself.

PASS THE SALAD

When the winter doldrums hit you in mid-January, do you crave a nice, fresh green salad? If you have those cravings once in awhile, you probably realize your body is telling you it needs something nutritionally from that salad. Cats often crave greens, too, and for the same reason.

Cats allowed to go outside will munch on grass or certain weeds in the backyard, but indoor cats will need some help to satisfy those cravings. Most pet supply stores carry cat salad kits that you can grow at home. They usually consist of a small pot with potting soil and seeds. Dampen the soil, plant the seeds and in a few days they will sprout. When they are a few inches high, trim the greens with a sharp pair of scissors and offer them to your cat. She will probably gobble them down! Every other day or so, trim the grass and give your cat a treat. You can also put the pot on the floor from time to time and let you cat graze like a sheep. You may even want to keep two or three pots growing so you have an on-going supply. Don't let your cat have free access to the grass, though, because she will probably rip the grass up by the roots, killing it. She may also over-indulge, giving herself a tummy ache.

You can bring your cat in some of the grass from your backyard, as long as you are absolutely positive the grass is clean and free from pesticides, insecticides, and fertilizers. Just trim a small handful of new green grass and offer it to your cat. She'll probably love it.

Wheat grass and oat grass are commonly sold for cats.

CATNIP

Catnip is an herb in the mint family. Some cats are so attracted to catnip that they will do anything for it, including opening cupboard doors, scratching through bags, and meowing so pathetically that you give up and give them some. Other cats don't seem attracted or affected by it at all.

Cats affected by catnip could have one or more amusing reactions. Some roll in the herb, lick it, or eat it. Some purr, growl, meow, or chitter. The catnip makes some cats very relaxed, while it stimulates others. Some get very playful, while others get downright aggressive.

Catnip is easy to grow, in a pot or in your garden.

If your cat has a pleasant reaction to catnip, you can buy the dried herb at pet supply stores and sprinkle it on her toys or on her scratching post or tree. You can also grow catnip in the garden outside or in a pot on the windowsill. If you grow it outside, don't be surprised if all of the neighborhood cats discover your garden! If you grow your own catnip, offer your cat just a single new leaf or blossom at a time; many cats react much more strongly to fresh catnip than dried.

Catnip is perfectly safe for your cat. However, like any treat, the thrill fades if it is offered too often. For maximum pleasure, give your cat catnip just once or twice a week. The same goes for catnip toys. They quickly lose their special allure if they are available all the time. So pick up the catnip toys and put them away in a drawer after your cat has finished playing. When you bring them out again, they'll be exciting in a whole new way for your cat.

YOU CAN TRAIN A CAT

Most cat owners react to the idea of training a cat with surprise. "Train a cat? Yeah, right! My cat trains me." That's probably true. Cats are very intelligent (more than we give them credit for), and are very good at teaching us to do what they want us to do. However, training your cat is a good idea and is not nearly as difficult as you might think.

Training your cat to respond to certain things can make life with your cat safer and more fun. For example, your cat should recognize her name and respond when you call her. She should learn where she is allowed to be and what spots are off-limits to her. She should learn where she is allowed to scratch (her cat tree) and that she is not to scratch the furniture. She can learn to ride in a carrier and even to walk on a harness and leash. You can also teach her some tricks if you (and she) agree.

You cannot train a cat using force. If you try to force a cat to do something, or use harsh training techniques, you will scare your cat and teach her to distrust you. However, cats are easily trained using positive reinforcements. A positive reinforcement is something the cat likes that you can use to reward her cooperation. For example, if your cat likes to be scratched behind the ears, an ear scratch can be positive reinforcement. A furry mouse toy, special treats, and verbal praise can all be positive

A cat won't heel on a leash the way a dog will. You'll have to let your cat lead you if you want to take her out for walks.

reinforcements, too. The key is to use something you know for sure your cat likes.

When your cat does something right, use your voice to praise her, "Good girl Kitty! Yeah, what a smart cat!" and give her the treat or toy as you continue to praise her. For example, if you want to teach your cat to come when she's called, get out that special toy or treat and let your cat see it and smell it. Say her name, "Kitty!" in a happy tone of voice to get her attention. Then back up a step or two, holding the toy or treat so that your cat can see it as you tell her, "Kitty, come!" When your cat moves toward you, praise her and give her the treat. Only do this two or three times per training session, and then stop. Cats do not do well with repetition and are easily bored. You can practice again a few hours later. Gradually increase the distance you ask your cat to come to you.

You can also use that special reinforcement as a lure. To teach your cat to ride in the carrier, prop the door open and toss the treat inside, saying, "Kitty, go in! Good girl!" Let her go in to get the treat and come back out on her own. When your cat is very comfortable going in and out on her own after the treat, put her food bowl in the carrier for a few meals (you are using her food as a lure and as positive reinforcement). When she eats in there comfortably, close the door while she's eating. When she's OK with that, pick the carrier up and carry it around the house (with the door closed, and after she's finished eating).

TEACHING YOUR CAT

When you want to teach your cat something new, think about the following:

O What is it you want to teach her?
O What name or command do you wish to use for this behavior?
O What lure or positive reinforcement will your cat react to?
O How can you help her figure out what you want?
O How can you reward her for doing it?

Keep the training as positive as possible and you will continue to keep your cat's cooperation!

BOUNDARY TRAINING

For your cat's safety, it's important that she learn what areas are off limits. For example, the stove is obviously a dangerous place and she should never jump up onto it. Some other places that you might want to put off limits include:

○ All kitchen counters, including the sink and the microwave
○ The washing machine and dryer, especially inside the dryer
○ High book shelves or knick-knack shelves
○ The dining room table
○ Hanging potted plants
○ Trash cans
○ Doors that open to the outside world

One of the easiest ways to train your cat to stay away from or off certain places is by using a squirt bottle or a child's water pistol. Fill a squirt bottle with water and set it next to you on the sofa. When your cat comes sauntering in and jumps up on the book shelves, giver her a squirt. Aim for the rump (there's no need to squirt her in the face). Once she jumps down, stop the correction immediately – don't hold a grudge. Instead, ignore her as she cleans that icky water off herself. Your cat will learn that venturing into or onto certain places will earn her a spray of water.

For a correction to be effective, you must catch your cat in the act. Even a few seconds later, she'll have no idea what she is being corrected for. So keep your squirt gun or spray bottle handy during the initial stages of boundary training.

Notice that with this technique, you aren't making a big deal out of it. There's no yelling, no forceful corrections, no anger – just a squirt of water.

When your cat makes a decision to NOT venture into or onto one of these spots, make sure you praise her. For example, if she walks into the living room, looks at the shelves, squats as if she's going to jump, thinks about it and then turns away – praise her! "Good Kitty! Yeah, good girl!" Pet her and give her one of her special treats. Let her know that you saw her make the right decision. She'll remember that reaction from you and will learn from it.

This kind of boundary training is enough for many cats. But if yours is one of the sneaky ones who stays off the kitchen counters when you're there to supervise but leaves little paw prints all over them while you sleep, try covering them with something she doesn't like. A sheet of aluminum foil works well – cats just hate to walk on it. Your cat will soon learn that even in your absence, the counters are no fun.

Tin foil or large rocks over the soil of your house plants will keep kitty out of the pot. And a mild vinegar and water solution sprayed on the leaves should deter chewing.

NO SCRATCHING!

Cats need to scratch, and you must give them someplace acceptable to do it. Cats scratch to pull off the outside worn layer of their claws. In addition, your cat will scratch to mark territory. She will stand on her rear legs and stretch up as high as she can reach to scratch. If she were outside, another cat might come along later and do the same thing. Whoever is taller and can reach higher is the winner! Scratching also provides a means of stretching the body. As your cat reaches, she will grab the scratching post (or your furniture or curtains) and then will stretch, arching her back. Last but certainly not least, cats scratch because they like to! It's a natural behavior and they enjoy doing it.

To prevent damage to your drapes and furniture, give your cat one or two scratching posts or cat trees. The ones covered with carpet or wrapped with sisal rope work well. The most interesting ones have different kinds of surfaces. Make sure the post or tree is tall enough so that your cat can reach upwards with her front paws – above her head – and still have room to stretch and grab. If the tree is too short, she may decide to use your taller furniture.

You can make the cat tree exciting by sprinkling it with catnip. Do so liberally in the beginning when your cat is just learning to use the cat tree. Later, you can sprinkle the catnip on the tree every once in awhile – just enough to keep your cat interested. Placement will also make the cat tree interesting. Remember, cats use their scratching post to mark territory. If you put it away in the basement or behind the couch, that is not territory worth marking. Your cat will choose a piece of furniture in a more worthy spot: where most of the family spends their time, and usually at the entrance to the main room.

If your cat has already decided to use a piece of furniture as a scratching post, you can change her mind. First, cover the spot on the furniture that she likes to scratch with something that might deter your cat. A piece of plastic carpet runner with the little knobs outward will work. So will aluminum foil. A towel scented with vinegar often works. So does double-sided tape. Once you have found something that will deter your cat, use it for several weeks while you are re-training her to use the cat tree instead.

If you catch your cat in the act of scratching, the water squirt correction works very well, but you have to have it close at hand. Don't run to grab the squirt bottle and then chase the cat down the hallway with it, trying to squirt her! She'll have no idea what she is being corrected for. Instead, if you know your cat likes to stretch and scratch immediately after eating her evening meal, have the squirt bottle close by at that time. When your cat walks up to that piece of furniture, wait until she reaches up with her front paws, then squirt her! As she dashes away, just ignore her – no more corrections.

If your cat is bound and determined to scratch your furniture and you haven't been able to stop her, you may want to look into nail caps or nail shields. These are covers that are glued onto the nails of the front feet and prevent the cat from doing any damage when she scratches. Most cats dislike the covers intensely when they're first applied, but usually get used to them. The shields must be re-applied each time your cat sheds her claws (about every six weeks or so) and sometimes can be difficult to apply.

Some cat owners resort to surgical declawing as a means of controlling scratching. Declawing involves the surgical removal of the cat's front nails, including the last toe bone. An alternative surgery consists of cutting the tendon that enables the cat to extend her nails. Both of these surgeries are expensive, very painful, and take away the cat's ability to defend herself and to express pleasure by kneading with her claws. Surgery should be a last resort *only after every other option has been tried,* and should *never* be used on a cat allowed to go outside.

KEEP YOUR CAT ACTIVE

Cats are not nearly as active as dogs are. In fact, some researchers estimate wild cats sleep about sixteen hours each day! Most cat owners will agree cats do enjoy their nap time. Even though your cat is an expert at napping, she still needs regular exercise. Exercise keeps her body healthy, her mind sharp, and most important, uses up some of that excess energy that might otherwise get her into trouble. The bored cat, the cat with too much energy, may be shredding furniture, knocking things off the shelves, dumping over the trash can, and much, much more.

Some cats, especially kittens, will run laps around the house, up and over the furniture, around the dining room table, and off the walls when they need exercise, but others will need some motivation to move around. That means you need to get involved.

Many cat toys are made with exercise in mind. Toys that are tied to a pole are good fun for cats. A small pole (usually made of fiberglass or plastic has a string or nylon cord fastened to it with a toy on the end. That toy might be a feather or two, a fur toy, or something that flutters when it moves. You can then tease your cat with this by dragging the toy along the floor, and when your cat leaps for it, a flick of the pole sends the toy away. Make sure you let your cat win once in awhile; if she loses all the time she'll stop playing. Your cat will run, stalk, creep, jump, and leap while playing with this toy – all good exercise.

Another great cat toy is a handheld small red laser dot that you can move all around, shining the light on the floors or the walls. A narrow-beam flashlight will also work. Many cats will chase this for a long time. Make sure you only use the lasers made specifically for cats. Many of the other small lasers, including laser pointers, can cause eye damage if the cat looks into the light.

Chase is another good game to play with your cat. Simply stalk her until she starts to run, then chase her around the house. Many cats love a good chase, and will run and hide, then come back again and again for another chase.

THERE'S NO SUBSTITUTE FOR YOU

Leave some small toys, such as a little ball or a furry mouse, around for you cat to play with any time. But you must make time at least once a day to play with your cat. She'll look forward to it; many anticipate it so much that they bring a toy to their owner! Especially if you keep your cat indoors, you must make sure she spends time every day running around and keeping her lithe cat body healthy and fit. This playtime is not only good exercise for your cat, but is a great bonding time for both of you.

TWO CAN PLAY

There are a lot of games you can play with your cat. It just takes a little imagination to figure out which games you both enjoy.

TRACK BALL TOYS

These are toys made for the cat to play with by herself, but many cats will play longer with some company. These toys have a ball that rolls around inside a closed circular track. There are openings where the cat can insert a paw and pat the ball. You can play, too, by flicking the ball with one finger to get it rolling quickly. Your cat will pat the ball back to you and you can go back and forth, trying to see who can pat the ball the hardest or the fastest. Watch out, though – your cat's paw is probably much faster than your finger!

MILK JUG TOY

This homemade toy is a lot of fun. Wash out an empty plastic gallon milk jug. Cut a few circular openings in the jug – big enough for your cat's paw and leg (but too small for her head to fit through) – then drop a ping pong ball or a catnip toy in the jug. To start the play, show your cat the toy and move it around. As your cat figures it out, she'll start batting the toy around. Your job will then be to put the toy back in the jug each time she fishes it out.

CARDBOARD BOX CASTLE

Cats love to sit in any box, and simply placing a box in each room of your house will be a great treat for your cat. But you can make things even more interesting by cutting a couple of windows in a cardboard box. Then turn the box over so that the closed end is on top. Invite your cat to crawl into the upended box. Use a feather or other toy to tease your cat at the windows. See who is the fastest: your cat in catching the feather or you in getting the feather away from your cat. Just make sure you let her get the toy now and then, or the game will quickly become boring.

WHAT'S UNDERNEATH?

Any toy instantly becomes more interesting when it's partially hidden. Put an old towel or a tablecloth on the floor, and then make a toy disappear under it. The sight of the toy disappearing, and the motion under the towel, will likely drive you cat to pounce with joy.

HAVOC PLAYS HIDE AND SEEK
Havoc, a gray domestic shorthair cat, likes to play hide and seek. I started by teaching him to come when I call him, and he's very reliable about responding to his name. He's not so excited by treats, so his positive reinforcements are verbal praise and petting. Both are very important to him, so they work just fine. I started teaching him the game by calling him when I'm in a different room. I would make a big fuss over him when he found me. He caught on quickly to the fact that this was a game, and would either sneak up on me when he found me or would pounce on me. I can now hide in closets, or behind doors, or cover myself with blankets and Havoc can still find me.

ENVIRONMENTAL ENRICHMENT

Environmental enrichment is a fancy term for making your cat's house more exciting. As much as you might enjoy playing with your cat, you won't be able to amuse her all the time. An exciting, interesting environment can help amuse her when you cannot.

CAT TREE

I mentioned a cat tree when I talked about scratching on the furniture. A cat tree can be much more than just a scratching post, though. Cat trees are available with shelves and tunnels to climb and play on. The cat tree could have a toy or two stashed in one of the beds or holes (depending upon how the tree is built). It could be sprinkled with catnip, or could have a feather dangling on a string.

WINDOW PERCH

Looking out the window is a form of cat TV. Build a shelf under a window that overlooks your yard or street. A piece of old carpet will make it easy to jump up on and an old towel will make it comfortable. Make sure the window and screen are very secure before you allow your cat access to the perch. If you can, mount one perch where it will catch the morning sun and one where the afternoon sun will hit. Your cat will quickly learn where she can bask in the sun.

Cats naturally like to be above it all, where they can survey their surroundings. A multi-level cat tree and window perches will help satisfy that need and keep your cat off the china cabinet.

WILD BIRD FEEDERS

A wild bird seed feeder and a hummingbird feeder could provide two good things at once: you are feeding the wild birds while amusing your cat. Just put the feeders outside a window where your cat can watch. The birds will quickly realize they are safe from your cat and will eat contentedly at the feeders.

MAKE A TENT

Throw an old towel over the coffee table or pull the tablecloth down to the floor on one side. You will be amazed at how quickly your cat gets into this "tent." In the wild, cats like to stay hidden as they stalk their prey, and then pounce at the last moment. Being in this tent is a lot like hunting to your cat. She'll pounce out from the tent to "kill" her toys, then run and hide again.

ROTATE THE TOYS

Even the most amusing toys can get boring after awhile. Put some of your cat's toys away and bring out others. Rotate the toys so they are constantly changing. This prevents boredom.

With a little imagination, you can find a host of other things to amuse your cat. A paper cup with a little canned cat food smeared inside on the bottom of the cup will keep your cat occupied for quite a while. A little catnip rubbed into a tennis ball will keep you laughing! A simple paper grocery bag is great fun, too. Think safety, of course, but use your imagination. Your cat will love it!

TEACH YOUR CAT A TRICK

Think cats aren't smart enough to learn tricks? The fact that they've convinced us they can't be trained shows just how smart they are! But learning tricks is all a matter of motivation. If you use positive reinforcements, it's relatively easy to teach a cat a few tricks. The key is to use positive reinforcements your cat likes (special treats or a favorite toy) and to keep training sessions very short. As I mentioned earlier, cats get bored easily, so don't practice a trick more than four or five times. Stop, do something else, then come back to it for a few more tries.

SIT UP

Either sit on the floor with your cat or invite her up on a chair or table. Let her watch you for a moment as you fiddle with her treats. Hopefully, as she watches you, she will sit. If she doesn't, maneuver a treat over and behind her head; as she follows it with her eyes, she will sit down. (You can add the command, "Kitty, sit!" and stop here. It's already an accomplishment to teach your cat to sit on command.)

Once she sits, let her see and sniff the treat. As she sniffs it, raise it above her head as you tell her "Kitty, sit up!" When her front paws lift off the ground as she stretches up, praise her and give her the treat. As she learns what you want, you can ask her to sit up higher or for a slightly longer period of time.

WAVE

With your cat in front of you, show her a treat but hold it out of reach. When she reaches for it with a front paw, tell her "Kitty, wave!" and praise her. When she is reaching out with the paw reliably, start refining the wave by moving your hand back and forth with the treat. For example, if you want her to wave high, move the treat higher and have her reach out higher.

SPIN

Let your cat see and sniff her treat. Then tell her, "Kitty, spin!" and lead her with the treat in a small circle in front of you. As she learns the trick and will do it willingly, make it faster or add circles so that she can spin more than once.

Trick training for cats may seem strange to some cat owners. After all, tricks are for dogs, right? Try it, though, and you'll be surprised at how much fun your cat will have once she figures it out. Your cat will enjoy the treats, the physical activity, the mental stimulation, and best of all, the attention she's getting from you.

CATS GROOM THEMSELVES

Keeping clean is serious business to a cat, and cats spend several hours a day grooming. If you have ever been licked by a cat's sandpaper tongue, you know that tongue is very different from your own. Your cat's tongue has thousands of tiny barbs called papillae. These papillae enable the cat to clean herself thoroughly, with the tiny barbs hooking onto the dead hair, flakes of skin, dirt, and parasites that might be in her coat. This tongue also cleans bits of food from the cat's paws and chest. If there is something sticky in her coat, something that doesn't want to come out with licking, your cat may try to nibble it out, using her front teeth to free it from her coat.

The cat is able to reach almost every part of her body to clean herself because she has a very flexible spine. If you watch a cat give herself a bath and then you try to duplicate some of the positions she can get

herself into with no trouble whatsoever, you won't be able to do it. People, even very flexible people, just can't bend or move the way a cat can. This flexibility enables her to reach just about every part of her body so that she can maintain the state of cleanliness that cats treasure.

Even those parts of the body that your cat cannot reach with her tongue will still be cleaned. She will lick a front paw, getting it slightly damp, and then rub that paw over her face, her ears, behind her ears, and even behind her head. She'll then bring the paw back to her mouth, clean it, and repeat the entire process until she's satisfied.

CLEANING CAN BE DANGEROUS

Because your cat cleans herself using her tongue (and sometimes her teeth), if she gets something toxic on her feet or fur she could poison herself. Many cats have died because they walked through spilled antifreeze and then washed their paws. Many other substances, including paints, paint thinners, fertilizers, insecticides, herbicides, and other commonly used chemicals, can kill your cat if she cleans herself after exposure to them. Use these chemicals carefully, and if you think your cat has been exposed to them quickly and immediately give her a bath, washing the substances off her body. Don't forget to clean her paws. Then call your veterinarian to see if a visit to the vet is needed.

YOUR ROLE IN GROOMING

WHAT ON EARTH IS A HAIRBALL?

When your cat grooms herself, she will swallow the dead hair that comes out of her coat. It might be wiser to spit out that hair, but that's not what cats do. Instead, the hair passes through the digestive system and, if all is well, is eliminated in the feces. However, if the cat is shedding heavily the hair might form a ball in the cat's stomach, creating a hairball. If the hairball is small, it might still move through the digestive system with no difficulty. But if it is larger, it could cause an intestinal blockage, requiring veterinary attention and sometimes even surgery. Most often, though, hairballs are thrown up. If you see a yellowish foamy puddle with an ugly, hairy thing in the middle of it, that's a hairball.

BRUSHING AND COMBING

Brushing and combing your cat can help prevent hairballs by cutting down on the amount of dead hair your cat swallows. It will also cut down on the amount of cat hair on your couch, your carpet and your clothes. Brushing also helps keep your cat's skin and coat healthy; even though she was made to groom herself, she can't take care of herself alone. You cat still needs your help. Regular grooming also enables you to examine your cat so that you can make sure she's healthy.

The types of brushes and combs you will need depend upon the type of coat your cat has. Shorthaired cats need a slicker brush to go through the coat all over the body, and a soft bristle brush for the short hair on the face and legs. If you are having trouble with fleas, you might want a flea comb as well. During shedding season, a shedder blade (like a horse's curry comb) is very effective at pulling out the dead hairs.

Use a comb around your cat's face and ears; a brush can scratch her delicate eyes, nose, and ears.

Always brush your cat in the direction in which her hair grows.

Longhaired cats will need a comb with longer tines to work through the long, fine hair, as well as a pin brush. Depending on the thickness of your cat's coat, you might still be able to use a slicker brush and a soft bristle brush.

Comb

If your cat develops matts (solid hair tangles), you may be able to de-tangle the hair by gently undoing the matt with your fingers. Once you have some of the tangles undone, you can comb the matt out. Hold

Pin brush

the hair in your fingers between the tangle and the cat's skin so you don't pull on the hair as you comb it. You can also trim it out using round-nosed scissors. Again, hold the hair in your fingers between the tangle and the skin so that you don't cut the cat's skin.

Try to set up a routine for combing and brushing your cat. Brush your longhaired cat every day. Brush your shorthaired cat at least once or twice a week. Start when your cat is a kitten, so that grooming will become a pleasurable part of her life. Having a routine will ensure that you do it regularly. In addition, your cat, being a creature of habit, will look forward to those grooming sessions.

As you comb and brush your cat, keep in mind that she's very small, but is extremely well-armed. Be gentle, move slowly, and keep the grooming session pleasant. If your cat lays back her ears, growls, hisses, bares her teeth, or swats at you with claws out, that means you have done something wrong. Either something hurts, you've pushed her too fast or too far, or you haven't been gentle enough. Don't get angry at your cat – she's only trying to communicate. Instead, back up, slow down, and try to see where the problem is.

THE HANDS-ON EXAM

After you've combed or brushed your cat, give her a full-body massage. With your fingers, gently massage over her head and around her ears, then down to and around her neck. Work down the neck to her shoulders, the rib cage, and chest. Then gently rub each front leg and paw, moving slowly and very, very gently. Go back up to her body, massage her back, hips and abdomen, then her back legs and even her tail.

During this massage you will be relaxing your cat, but in addition you will be getting to know her body. It's important that you know what is normal and what is abnormal so that should a problem arise, you will catch it early and be able to tell the veterinarian about it. For example, if you find a lump under the skin on the cat's ribcage, you will be able to tell your vet that you massaged your cat Friday evening and the lump wasn't there, but when you massaged her Sunday it was. You can also let him know whether it is painful for your cat, feels hot, moves under your fingers, or any other details that could help your veterinarian diagnose and treat your cat.

When you massage your cat, start when she's already relaxed. Don't try to force a cat to accept the massage when she's in the middle of playing; that is sure to fail! Instead, when your cat is asleep on your lap or curled up next to you, begin by petting her slowly and gently. When she begins to purr, start massaging her slowly and gently.

Some cats will protest the handling of certain body parts. If your cat dislikes having her paws touched, for example, you can desensitize her. During the massage, gently touch one paw, softly and quickly, and then go back to rubbing her head. Later, touch that paw again, briefly and softly, and reward her by rubbing another place she likes. (Most cats especially liked being scratched behind the ears and under the chin – places that are hard to reach when they groom.) By associating the touch on the paw with good rubbing, she will learn to tolerate it. Continue the desensitization over a long period of time. Don't rush it.

EYES, EARS, AND NAILS

During your massage and exam, look at your cat's eyes. They should be bright and shiny with no matter in them. A little matter in the corner of the eyes after sleep is natural, but continual matter or a discolored

Never pour ear cleaner directly into the ear canal.

Expose the nail by gently pressing the toe pad.

Cut the nail using a firm, quick stroke.

discharge should be brought to your veterinarian's attention.

Check your cat's ears, too, by peeking into each ear as you rub your cat's head. The ears should be clean and it should smell damp but not bad. If the ear has a cheesy or yeasty smell, an infection might be smoldering inside. Again, call your veterinarian. If there is a little dirt in the ear, you can gently wipe the ear with a cotton ball, or with a cotton ball dipped in witch hazel or a commercial ear cleaning solution. If the insides of the ears are very discolored, with a lot of waxy buildup that appears to have some blood or red flecks in it, your cat might have ear mites. Don't clean the ears if you suspect mites; take your cat to the veterinarian right away. He needs to see the discharge and then he will tell you how to treat the problem.

Check your cat's nails, too. You may wish to regularly trim the tips off of those razor-sharp weapons, as well. You can extend the cat's nails one at a time by putting your index finger on the pad of the foot below the nail and gently pressing downward with your thumb above the nail. If your cat's nail is white, you'll see the pink quick inside the nail. With a pair of feline nail clippers, simply snip off the tip of the nail, being careful not to cut into the quick. If the nail is black, cut the tip just where it starts to turn down. If your cat fusses about having her nails clipped, trim just one paw a day. Then give her a treat afterwards and tell her what a good girl she is.

THE FELINE SENSES

Cats are amazing animals. They can see in the dark, can hear the pitter-patter of a mouse's steps, and twist their bodies into astounding shapes. Is it any wonder that the ancient Egyptians and Aztecs worshipped them?

AMAZING SIGHT

Cats are very visual and in fact, depend upon their sense of sight more than any other sense. Although people can see stationary objects much better than cats can, cats can see movement much better than we can – which would make sense for a predator. Cats also have better peripheral vision than people have. While color is not important to cats (any color mouse will do), tests have shown that cats can see color, although they do have trouble distinguishing between shades of greens and yellows.

The cat's most important skill, for a hunter anyway, is her ability to see so well in the dark. She has big eyes with pupils that open all the way, letting in the maximum amount of light. And a layer of reflective cells behind the retina bounce light back through the retina to that the maximum amount of information is extracted from each image the cat sees. So while a cat can't see in total darkness, she needs very little light to see quite well.

AMAZING HEARING

Even though vision is her most important sense, your cat still has incredible hearing. By rotating her ears, which can each swivel independently almost one hundred

THE INNER EAR AND BALANCE

The ears are responsible for more than just hearing. They also contribute to the cat's incredible sense of balance. Although many cat owners think the cat's long tail gives her such excellent balance, even short-tailed or bob-tailed cats have very good balance. Instead, cats rely on an organ of balance in the inner ear called the vestibular apparatus, which instantly registers changes in velocity or orientation. That, coupled with the cat's quick reflexes, gives her the ability to right herself or balance in ways that simply take our breath away.

and eighty degrees, the outer ear flap helps the cat locate the direction of sounds. Watch your cat listening, and you'll see her ears sweeping the room like radar dishes. In addition, cats can hear almost two full octaves above what people can hear. This is even higher than the sounds dogs can hear.

CATS JUST DO IT!

Have you ever watched your cat jump from one piece of furniture to another and held your breath, thinking she wasn't going to make it? But she did it, didn't she? How do they do that? Part of the cats' amazing grace and balance comes from how they are made and put together. Let's face it, cats are the ultimate athletes. They are powerful and strong, with quick reflexes and wonderful balance. But that isn't all of it. Cats have an extra edge: They just know they can do it. When your cat jumps to the top of the refrigerator, she doesn't think about it. She doesn't ask herself, "Hmmm, I wonder if I can do that?" She just does it. She knows she can.

Where does this confidence come from? Part of it comes from just being a cat; she is who she is. But another part of it comes from her play. Kittens and cats leap, dash, run, jump, twist, and turn while they play. This play is fun, certainly, but it is also practice for life. While playing, your cat learns what she can do and what she cannot do. She learns what works and what doesn't work. She makes her clumsy moves, bad jumps, and inelegant leaps while playing. Then, when she tries to jump for real, she knows exactly how to do it.

YOUR CAT'S VACCINATIONS

Your new cat or kitten should go in to meet your veterinarian as soon as possible after you bring her home. At this first visit, your vet can examine the cat and establish her health status. He will look for any obvious health problems, including any signs of disease or genetic health defects, such as ear mites or cataracts. If, during the exam, the vet does find a problem, he can advise you about how to deal with it.

Your vet will also want to know what vaccinations your cat has been given and when, so that he can set up a vaccination schedule. The vaccinations given most often include:

○ **Feline panleukopenia:** This virus is highly contagious and is spread through bodily fluids.

○ **Feline leukemia (FeLV):** This retrovirus is transmitted through bodily fluids.

○ **Feline infectious peritonitis (FIP):** This vaccine is relatively new and there are still questions regarding its use.

○ **Rabies:** The rabies virus is always fatal once contracted.

Your veterinarian may also recommend other vaccines, depending upon where you live, whether your cat lives indoors only or not, and what diseases have been seen in the area. They may include feline calicivirus (a respiratory virus), feline viral rhinotracheitis (another respiratory disease), and chlamydia psittaci (yet another respiratory disease).

WHAT ABOUT BOOSTER SHOTS?
There is some disagreement about how often a cat needs to be revaccinated against certain diseases. The traditional idea of booster shots every year is no longer endorsed by every veterinarian, and there is some research to suggest it might not be the best thing for your cat. New studies are being done all the time, and this is an area where we still have much to learn. Some veterinary schools are now recommending revaccination every three years.

Talk to your veterinarian about the vaccinations he recommends and what schedule your cat should follow. If you have questions about specific diseases or the vaccinations, ask him about them. After all, the more you know, the easier it will be for you to make sure your cat gets the best care.

THE ANNUAL CHECK-UP

A healthy cat should still see the veterinarian once a year for a check-up. This visit is a chance for the vet to look your cat over, to make sure your cat is healthy and to check for potential problems. Cats have great fortitude, and usually will not show any signs of disease until they are very sick. An annual check-up can help identify problems before they get serious.

Your vet may look at your cat's ears to check for signs of infection or mites. He will look at your cat's teeth to see whether any are broken. He will also check the teeth for tartar buildup. The veterinarian is not trying to find problems, but instead is making sure that nothing is wrong. However, if he does find a problem, it is better to find it early.

During the exam, ask any questions you might have about caring for your cat. Do you need help dealing with fleas? There are quite a few new products on the market. Ask your vet what he recommends for cats. Are you worried about heartworm? It has been seen in cats in some regions. Ask if you should put your cat on a preventive medication. Your vet will be more than willing to answer your questions, so ask away!

SIGNS OF HEALTH

○ **Attitude:** Willing to play; watchful, alert
○ **Energy level:** Appropriate to the cat's age; ready to play
○ **Eyes:** Bright and shiny, no discharge or cloudiness
○ **Ears:** Clean, with a damp but inoffensive smell
○ **Nose:** Damp, slightly cool, a slight clear discharge is normal
○ **Respiration:** Breath should smell OK; breaths should move in and out cleanly
○ **Grooming:** Regular, thorough grooming
○ **Teeth and gums:** Clean teeth with little or no tartar; gums tight to the teeth and pink; hearty appetite
○ **Skin:** Clean and clear
○ **Coat:** Clean, shiny, and healthy; shedding is reasonable, depending on the season
○ **Urination:** No difficulty or straining; urine clear
○ **Defecation:** No difficulty in defecating; feces solid and well-formed

It's important to see regular, steady weight gain in a growing kitten.

SIGNS OF ILLNESS

○ **Attitude:** A change in attitude; excess sleepiness; lack of attention
○ **Energy level:** A change in energy levels with no apparent reason; hyperactivity; inability to control self; total lack of energy; inability or lack of desire to do her favorite things
○ **Eyes:** Discharge, matter, crustiness, cloudiness
○ **Ears:** Dark wax, discharge, cheesy or yeasty smell
○ **Nose:** Dry and chapped, hot; opaque discharge; green, brown, or darker discharge
○ **Respiration:** Heavy breathing; panting, wheezing, inability to catch her breath; sounds of fluid in the lungs; coughing, sneezing
○ **Grooming:** Lack of grooming; a disheveled appearance
○ **Teeth and gums:** Tartar buildup; bleeding gums; red, inflamed gums; bad breath; loss of appetite
○ **Skin:** Redness, rash; flaking, itching skin; chewed spots, sores; scratching
○ **Coat:** Excessive shedding; dry, dull coat; bare spots
○ **Urination:** Any change from normal; difficulty or straining; frequent trips to the litter box; blood or cloudiness in urine
○ **Defecation:** Any change from normal; difficulty or straining; soft feces; blood in feces; diarrhea

Straining, or frequent trips to the litter box, are signs of a problem.

WHEN DOES YOUR CAT NEED TO GO TO THE VET?

Make an appointment to take your cat to the veterinarian as soon as possible if any of the following occurs:

○ **Signs of illness:** Your cat is displaying any of the signs of illness listed on page 53.
○ **Injuries:** Your cat has injured herself and is still limping an hour after the accident.
○ **Swelling:** Your cat has an unexplained swelling.
○ **Insect sting or bite, or animal bite:** Your cat was stung or bit by an insect or another animal.

Take your cat to the veterinarian right away (call first to let them know you're on the way) if any of the things listed below happen. If the office isn't open, take your cat to the emergency animal clinic.

○ **Respiratory distress:** Your cat is having trouble breathing or is choking.
○ **Bleeding:** Your cat has been injured and is bleeding.
○ **Insect sting or bite, or animal bite:** Your cat has been stung or bit, and is swelling or appears to be going into shock.
○ **Snake bite:** Your cat has been bitten by a snake. Be able to identify the snake, if it's at all possible.
○ **Poisons:** Your cat has touched, been exposed to, or has eaten a poison.
○ **Burns:** Your cat has been burned, either by exposure to heat or caustic chemicals.
○ **Electrical shock:** Your cat has been shocked, even if she now appears to be normal.

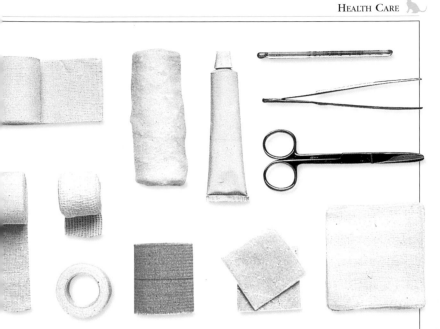

YOUR FELINE FIRST AID KIT

Keep these items on hand in a separate kit that you've set aside just for your cat. Make sure to look through it now and then, so you can replace items that have become old or outdated.

- ○ Rolls of gauze or fabric of different widths
- ○ Gauze pads of different sizes
- ○ Rolls of tape
- ○ Elastic to wrap around bandages
- ○ Antiseptic cleaning wipes
- ○ Alcohol prep pads
- ○ Bactine
- ○ Bacitracin ointment

- ○ Benadryl tablets
- ○ Kaopectate tablets or liquid
- ○ Hydrogen peroxide
- ○ Saline eye wash
- ○ Tweezers
- ○ Scissors
- ○ Disposable razors
- ○ Cat nail clippers
- ○ Comb and brush
- ○ An extra cat harness and leash

EMERGENCY FIRST AID

If your cat has been injured or suddenly taken ill, your quick response to the situation could save her life.

CPR

Feline cardiopulmonary resuscitation requires quick action to be effective.

○ If your cat has stopped breathing, place her on her side, open her mouth and pull the tongue to one side. Make sure the airway is clear.

○ If the mouth and airway are clear, close the mouth and place your hand completely around the cat's muzzle. Blow GENTLY into the cat's nose and watch for her chest to rise. Repeat twelve times per minute.

○ If the cat has no pulse, place three fingers over the heart (at about the fifth rib) and press gently but with medium pressure and then release. The ribs should compress about one inch. Repeat five times. (If the cat has a pulse but is not breathing, give assisted breathing only.)

○ Do twelve breaths, then five chest compressions, and repeat until your cat starts to breathe on her own.

SPLINT

A broken limb can be very painful. If at all possible, do not move the cat until you can splint the limb.

○ Use a ruler, a thick pencil or a stick. Ideally, the splint should be longer than the cat's leg.

○ Using gauze, wrap the splint to the leg. Do not attempt to straighten the leg – let the veterinarian do that.

○ Make sure the wrap does not cut off the flow of blood to the leg.

○ Take the cat to the veterinarian's office as soon as possible.

BLEEDING

Bleeding can be life-threatening.

O If the wound is oozing, use a gauze pad to put direct pressure on the wound until you arrive at the vet's office.

O If the wound is oozing continuously, put pressure on the wound with a towel or several gauze pads and consider it a serious emergency. Get to the vet's office right away.

O If the wound is spurting, a blood vessel has been broken and your cat could bleed to death. Use a shoelace or a length of gauze to make a tourniquet above the wound – between the wound and the heart. Wrap the tourniquet around the limb and then tie it to a pencil, pen, or small stick. Twist the stick so that it tightens the tourniquet until the bleeding slows. Get your cat to the vet's office immediately. If it takes longer than ten minutes to get to the vet's office, loosen the tourniquet every ten minutes to allow blood circulation to that limb.

Be aware that a tourniquet can create serious problems, because it cuts off all blood flow. Only use a tourniquet if direct pressure doesn't work and your cat is in danger of bleeding to death.

RESTRAINT

Cats that are frightened and hurt may try to hurt you – even your own cat. The easiest way to restrain a cat is to use a pillowcase. Simply scoop the cat up in the pillowcase, leaving only her head out. If you need to treat something on the cat's body, use a towel to wrap up the cat, covering her eyes and leaving uncovered the hurt part of the body. This will give you time to perform emergency first aid. Whenever you cover the cat's head, check frequently to make sure she can still breathe!

CARRYING YOUR CAT

Make sure when you carry your cat that you aren't making her injuries worse. Find something that you can slip under your cat (a board, the kitchen cutting board, or even a tray), slide that under her, moving her as little as possible, and then carry her to your car that way.

YOUR CAT NEEDS YOU

As I write these words, my gray domestic shorthaired cat, Havoc, is lying on my lap, purring loudly. Every once in awhile he shifts his weight, as if to remind me he's there. As if I could ignore his twenty pounds! If the keyboard tapping stops, he will lift his head and look at me with those lovely gold eyes. I think, as far as he's concerned, that if I'm not actually typing away at the keyboard, I should be petting him.

People who don't have cats seem to think that cats are aloof and standoff-ish. Any cat owner can tell you that cats are just the opposite; they are very affectionate, very loving, and very dependent upon their owners. Now, that doesn't mean cats are like dogs, because they aren't. A cat will not nudge you with her nose, then drop a ball in your lap and drool on your feet until you throw the ball. No, cats are more subtle than that. Cats want affection and lots of it, but they want it on their own terms. When Havoc wants attention, he will sit in the doorway and stare at me until I acknowledge him. When I do, he will meow in this teeny tiny voice and rub up against something – even the wall. If I tell him, "Come here, silly cat," he will wander over and place himself within reach so that I can pet him. If I do so just the way he likes, I will end up with a cat in my lap or draped over my shoulders.

As much as they are reluctant to admit it, our cats need us. They are domesticated and need us for good health care, vaccinations, and protection from illnesses and injuries. They need our protection from the world – both the wild world and the domesticated one. And we need them too. Cats always seem to know when we're sad or lonely or ill, and they make a special effort to be snuggly when we need them most. In our homes we can protect our cats, love our cats, and treasure them. And that's how it should be.

MORE TO LEARN

BOOKS

The Cat's Mind, by Bruce Fogle, DVM, Howell Book House

The Consumer's Guide to Cat Food, by Liz Palika, Howell Book House

The Encyclopedia of the Cat, by Bruce Fogle, DVM, Dorling Kindersley Publishing

The Encyclopedia of Natural Pet Care, by C. J. Puotinen, Keats Publishing

The Everything Cat Book, by Steve Duno, Adams Media Corp.

First Aid for Cats, by Tim Hawcroft, BVSc, MACVSc, Howell Book House

Housecat, by Christine Church, Howell Book House

Natural Cat Care, by Bruce Fogle, DVM, Dorling Kindersley Publishing

Roger Tabor's Cat Behavior: A Complete Guide to Understanding How Your Cat Works by Roger Tabor, Reader's Digest Books

Shelter Cats, by Karen Commings, Howell Book House

Think Like a Cat, by Pam Johnson-Bennett, Penguin

MAGAZINES

Cat Fancy
PO Box 6500
Mission Viejo, CA 92690
(714) 855-8822
www.catfancy.com

Cats & Kittens
7-L Dundas Circle
Greensboro, NC 27407
(336) 292-4047
www.catsandkittens.com

Cats Magazine
260 Madison Ave.
New York, NY 10016
(917) 256-2298
www.catsmag.com

WEB SITES

Alternative Veterinary Medicine
www.altvetmed.com

American Animal Hospital Association
www.healthypet.com

American Veterinary Medical Association
www.avma.org/care4pets

Cat Fanciers
www.fanciers.com

Cats! Wild to Mild
www.lam.mus.ca.us/cats/

Cornell Feline Health Center
web.vet.cornell.edu/Public/FHC

National Animal Poison Control Center • (888) 426-4435
www.napcc.aspca.org

NetVet
www.avma.org/netvet/cats.htm

The Pet Channel
www.thepetchannel.com

PogoPet
www.pogopet.com

Poisonous Plant Guide
www.ansci.cornell.edu/plants/plants.
html

Vaccines and Sarcomas
www.avma.org/vafstf/ownbroch.html

Wisconsin Cat Club
www.wicatclub.com

FELINE ASSOCIATIONS
Alley Cat Allies
1801 Belmont Rd. NW, Suite 201
Washington DC, 20009
(202) 667-3630 • www.alleycat.com

American Association of Cat
Enthusiasts
PO Box 213
Pine Brook, NJ 07058
(973) 335-6717 • www.aaceinc.org

American Association of
Feline Practitioners
2701 San Pedro NE, Suite 7
Albuquerque, NM 87110
(505) 888-2424 •www.avma.org/aafp

American Cat Fanciers Association
PO Box 203
Point Lookout, MO 65726
(417) 334-5430 • www.acfacat.com

Canadian Cat Association
220 Advance Blvd., Suite 101
Brampton, Ontario L6T 4J5, Canada
(905) 459-1481 • www.caa-afc.com

Cat Fancier's Association
1805 Atlantic Ave.
Manasquan, NJ 08736-0805
(908) 528-9797 • www.cfainc.org

Cat Fancier's Federation
PO Box 661
Gratis, OH 45330
(513) 787-9009 • www.cffinc.org

The International Cat Association
PO Box 2684
Harlingen, TX 78551
(956) 428-8046 • www.tica.org

VIDEOS
Incredible Cat Tricks, with animal
trainer Karen Payne. • Available from
most online video stores and many
pet supply stores

Your Cat Wants a Massage, with
massage therapist Maryjean Ballner.
Available from Cat Massage Works,
4061 East C.V. Blvd. Suite 4, Castro
Valley, CA 94552-4840, (877) MEOW-
MEOW • www.catmassage.com

ABOUT THE AUTHOR

Liz Palika and her husband Paul share their home with three
domestic shorthaired cats, Havoc, Squirt, and Troubles. All three
cats were rescued. Havoc, her littermates and mother were
abandoned in a box outside a local business. Squirt was found (as
a kitten) roaming around a local shopping center, and Troubles
was picked up from the center divider of a freeway. Today all are
happy, healthy, and rule the Palika household – much to the
dogs' dismay! Liz is an award-winning author whose book, *The
Consumer's Guide to Cat Food*, won the Cat Writers Association
Special Award on Nutrition, sponsored by Purina, in 1997.

INDEX

Dorling Kindersley

LONDON, NEW YORK, SYDNEY, DELHI, PARIS,
MUNICH, JOHANNESBURG

Project Editor: Beth Adelman
Design: Carol Wells
Layout: Annemarie Redmond, Gus Yoo
Photo Research: Mark Dennis
Index: Nanette Cardon

Photo Credits: Jane Burton, Steve Gorton, Dave King, Tim Ridley

First American Edition, 2000
2 4 6 8 10 9 7 5 3 1

Published in the United States by
Dorling Kindersley Publishing, Inc. 95 Madison Avenue New York, New York 10016

Dorling Kindersley Publishing, Inc. offers special discounts for bulk purchases for sales promotion
or premiums. Specific, large-quantity needs can be met with special editions, including
personalized covers, excerpts of existing guides, and corporate imprints. For more information,
contact Special Markets Department, Dorling Kindersley Publishing, Inc.,
95 Madison Avenue, New York, NY 10016 Fax: (800) 600-9098.

Color reproduction by Colourscan, Singapore
Printed in Hong Kong by Wing King Tong

Library of Congress Cataloging-in-Publication Data
Palika, Liz, 1954-
    What your cat needs / Liz Palika.— 1st American ed.
        p. cm. — (What your pet needs)
Includes index.
    ISBN 0-7894-6308-3 1. Cats. I. Title. II. Series.
    SF447 .P35 2000
    636.8—dc21
    00-008260

See our complete catalog at
www.dk.com